Kangaroo Unbound

© 2025 Luke Johnson

This book is copyright. Apart from any fair dealing for the purposes of study and research, criticism, review or as otherwise permitted under the Copyright Act, no part may be reproduced by any process without written permission. Inquiries should be made to the publisher.

First published in 2025
Published by Puncher & Wattmann
PO Box 279
Waratah NSW 2298

info@puncherandwattmann.com

A catologue record for this book is available from The National Library of Australia.

ISBN   9781923099623

Cover image by Garry Shead, *Flaming Kangaroo* 1992, oil on composition board, 91 x 121.5cm.

Cover design by David Musgrave

Printed by Lightning Source International

Kangaroo Unbound

Luke Johnson

PUNCHER & WATTMANN

*For Mara,
and Garry.*

The following poems take their titles and, to varying degrees, inspiration from Garry Shead's 'D.H. Lawrence' paintings. The paintings can be viewed at luke-johnson.com.au or by scanning the QR code below (with permission from the artist).

Contents

the arrival	1
The Conspirators	3
They Were There	4
Thirroul	6
Railway Station	8
Thirroulia	10
Free	12
kan / ga / roo	13
The Presence I	14
The Struggle	15
1922	16
Fame, or Portrait of the Artist as a Blue Triangle	17
The Visitors	18
(After) The Wave	20
Le Déjeuner sur l'Herbe	21
Aboriginal	23
Headland	24
Sentinel	26
The Cliff	27
The Letter	29
The Presence II	30
Dusk	31
The League	33
Nightfall	34
Nightfall II	35
A Father Is Greater than His Son (fka Firelight)	36
The Dream	40
The Guards	42
New Land	43
The Antipodes	44
The Rainbow	46
The Cockies	47

Flaming Kangaroo	48
Creation	50
The Dance	51
The Awakening	52
the awakening ii	55
The Envoy	57
Noon	58
Treason	59
The Secret	60
The Intruder	62
Marriage	63
Checkmate	64
Checkmate II	65
The Supper	68
The Meeting	69
Death of Cooley	70
Death of Kangaroo	72
The Monument	74
Main Street	75
The Apotheosis of D.H. Lawrence	76
Acknowledgements	77

the arrival

we wait
over an hour
for the poet
to arrive
at the bookstore
for the reading
we didn't want
to attend
in the first place
finally he appears
with a copy
of his own book
tucked under his own arm
yellow post-it notes
sticking up
out of the pages
at crazy
cockatoo-crested angles
to help him
locate the poems
he has determined
best suited
to the occasion
such as the one
about the obscure thing
no one's ever heard of
and the one
about the thing
everyone's heard of
but cannot make sense of
within the context
of the poem

and at long last
the one that finishes
with a rhyming couplet
that makes everyone laugh
and clap
with relief
especially his poor parents
who seated
two rows
in front of us
were clearly beginning
to wonder
what kind
of pointless imbecile
they had brought
into this world and
through how much more of this shit
was he expecting them to, er, sit.

The Conspirators

The   harbour

                                                      at

sunset

                      is a   conspiracy

of colour

and   movement.

                                    The

    water's

                  surface   ripples   like

an enormous   silk   flag.

                Bloodshed red

and   tourism

      blue   with   t w i n k l i n g s

               of windsail   white,

caught together   in the

     lunacy

of an outgoing

                                          tide.

They Were There

~

at the bottom of the steps
beneath the station platform
where the rail guards
have no jurisdiction
and the police
are as dimensionless
as clouds
floating reflectively
across the surface
of an imaginary lake,
a pair of Jehovah's Witnesses
stand in front
of a no smoking sign
hoping some
ciggy butt brain
might stop
and ask them for a light

~

holding hands
on the lawn
in front of
the McKinnon building
where pro-
Palestinian protestors
run poster-
making workshops
and future P.E. teachers
throw frisbees
at one another with
freakish ambidexterity,

a hoodie-wearing
collective of Christian
exchange students
give thanks for
God knows what

~

walking single-
file and shoeless
through Crown Street mall
early Saturday morning,
five Caucasian monks
from the nearby temple
appear blissfully unaware
of the way
their shiny white
craniums reflect the glow
of the newly
refurbished KFC outlet
located directly beneath
the out-
of-order escalator

Thirroul

Thirroul's gone to the
dogs, I tell you. Every
second shop's become a
lime-washed homewares
store, the mural of Jim
Morrison painted on
the wall next to the pub's
been photo-acoustically
removed, Jolly Roger's
fish and chip shop where
Steve worked back when
he still had dreadlocks and
couldn't surf for shit is
now a toddler friendly
Jiu-Jitsu studio ('they used
to sell Chiko Rolls, now
they roll chicos' – Steve's
joke, not mine; nice one,
Steve), it's pretty much
mayhem finding a park on
the street, while Buck
Hamblin's shoe store has
been transformed into a
     wait for it…
hipster café!! Locals blame
gentrification and the forces
of neocapitalism, but I
blame D.H. Lawrence. See,
no one knew gentrification
was even a thing before
Lawrence went and gave
some plucky young gamekeeper

a taste for upper-middle class
snatch, and now look where
we are for f—'s sake.

Railway Station

I was not there
to greet the Lawrences
when they disembarked
the 2 pm train
from Central Station
at Thirroul on
the 29th of May 1922
though I'd like
to think the mood
was much the same
that day as it was
today when waiting
on the same platform
with my earphones in
and collar up I
witnessed a schoolboy
pretend to throw himself
in front of a screaming
southbound freight train
for no reason other
than to terrify the
schoolgirl whose
hand he had been
holding and whose neck
he had been nuzzling
right up until he got
that dumb teenage look in
his eye and rushed forward
with her squealing and
rushing after him,
which is to say
a reckless albeit not

totally incomprehensible
sort of mood.

Thirroulia

A town is being born
but it's happening all wrong,
instead of dropping head-first
from the starry night sky like it's supposed to,
it's being squeezed up out of the earth in breech position,
with a bugle-eyed view
of the flailing footpaths, public orifices
and gaudy genitalia
that will shape its personality
for decades to come.

A town is being born
but not the way God or Nature intended,
it's coming through prematurely
– without its people,
just a mutinous, synaesthetic jangle
of fauna-infused flora
and flora-infused fauna
bulging perilously through weak points
in the queer topography of yesteryear
and the malnutritional layers of ozone
spread out over tomorrowyear.

A town is being born
but there's something queasy about the spectacle,
the way it thickens the air with flies
and makes the ground feel sticky underfoot,
like the emergence of sewerage following a storm
or the nightmarish visions
that proceed from digesting too much garlic
too close to bedtime,
no brolly-speckled shoreline or

Sunday promenades just yet,
only the violent surge of progesterone
that accompanies the miracle of reproduction:
the earth is being torn,
a name is being sworn,
Thirroulia! Thirroulia!
a town has just been born.

Free

You feel free in Australia. There
is great relief in the atmosphere
and you feel free. In Australia there
is great relief in the atmosphere
and you feel great. And free. Great
and free. All the time. And it is
free to feel great and free in Australia.
For Australia is free. And Australia
is great. And you feel the greatness
in the atmosphere and it is a great
relief. And you feel the freedom in
the atmosphere and it is a great
relief too. In Australia there is great
relief in the atmosphere and it is
the relief of feeling free. All the
time. And there is a feeling of
greatness that comes with feeling
so great all the time. And in Australia
it is in the atmosphere. This feeling
of greatness. And you feel it. You
really do. You feel it greatly. All
the time. And you need to feel it
greatly all the time too. For it is the
free-feeling feeling of being free.
Because to *be* free you need to *feel* free.
And in Australia you do. All the time. The
atmospheric feeling of both *being* and
feeling free. Of being and feeling free
right here. All the time. In free Australia.
In free Australia where you feel free
and great all the time. In free Australia
where you feel free and great and
full of need all the all-the-time.

kan / ga / roo

ayoungbuck / abroadforthe / firsttimeand
tipsyfromthe / beeratlunch / iwasapproached
byayoung / coupleresemblingdavid / andfriedalawrence
outsideapub / ontheshoreline / oflochlomond
whoaskedif / iwasinterested / inspendingthe
eveningwiththem / onthishouseboat / theyhadrented
andbeingthe / youngbucki / waswhichis
tosayvery / naïveandunworldly / andconfusedby
theexchangerates / nottomention / beingyouknow
fromaustraliawhere / wedonthave / lochsandwhere
wedrinkour / beerfromschooners / notpintsi
couldnotunderstand / whythisattractive / youngcoupleresembling
davidandfrieda / lawrenceshouldhave / wantedmeintruding
ontheirromantic / eveningtogetherand / sosaidno
thankyouand / insayingno / thankyoupassed
upwhati / seenowwas / probablythebest
opportunityiwill / evergetat / havingathreesome
withacouple / onahouseboat / onlochlomond

The Presence I

Old movies
lead me to believe
there was a time
when the sexiest thing
a woman could do
was sit by herself
in a monochromatic bar
full of businessmen
and jazz music
blowing cigarette smoke
upwards into her own eyes.

I think this
is because Sigmund
Freud's nephew
Edward Bernays
the war-time propagandist
cum father of public relations
had brainwashed
the men of this epoch
into believing
that a woman
willing to blow smoke
into her own eyes
would be only too happy
to blow a little
up her husband's arse
from time to time too.

The Struggle

is a concrete found poem where triangular blocks of text are used to track the proliferation of maternal desire and patricidal rivalry across interspecial kin groups in the mytho-figurative paintings of artist Garry Shead

is a problem

is a confirmation

is a lie which hides the presence of the External Mediator

is a bit like guilt

is a text that has been falsified

is unreal

is a gesture of Supreme Ambivalence

is a total

is a part

is a trickster of thought

is a crystallized, totemic precipitate of society

is a Concept Absolute

is a neurotic tic

1922

Wyewurk, Thirroul

the house smells of
dried botanicals arranged
in a ceramic milk bottle
and placed on a jarrah table
beside a small closed window
overlooking a nearby cliff
where the previous occupant,
a mother of eleven, dreamt daily
of throwing herself away

Fame or, Portrait of the Artist as a Blue Triangle

A real Johnson family portrait, this one:
you've got poor beetroot-headed ginger-
footed Dad, wobbling about all good-humouredly
like that Christmas Eve he decided to join
us in the front row of Church after knocking
off early with a case of Crown Lager at the
Holden dealership where he manned the spare
parts counter for a solid eighteen years; Mum
doing her best to keep him looking semi-decent,
semi-respectable, semi-upright, semi-sober in
front of Father Tony or Richard or Fred or Warren
or whichever one of them clerical oddities it was
up there presiding over the manger that year; and
me, not as I am now or was then, but rather as I
first appeared to the old girl in a prophetic, second-
trimestral dream, i.e. as a blue triangle of concern
being squeezed isosceles-wise through two
stirruped and bloody knees she recognised most
sagaciously and disturbedly as her own. As
you might expect, some of the details have been
exaggerated for artistic effect (in real life, my
mum isn't a red kangaroo, my dad avoids wearing
ties at all costs, I'm somewhat more scalene in
appearance if not nature, while the cheery
seaside vista bunged in around us to provide the
illusion of depth-of-field bears no resemblance
whatsoever to the lamb-flattened landscapes of
youth I keep thumb-tacked to the corky cortex
board in my head), but isn't this the whole point of
portraiture, anyhow – paying someone to locate all
your best, most flattering angles so they can be high-
lighted to the point of excruciating equilateralism?

The Visitors

Given their genetic proximity, the visitors,
    who arrive too punctually,
    travel with their own pillows,
    are on better terms with your neighbours than you are,
    prefer instant to real coffee,
    shower for the wrong length of time (too short),
    insist on calling lunch 'dinner' and dinner 'tea',
    enjoy watching TV with the volume muted,
    return from their nightly strolls with criminal quantities of plant clippings,
    care too little about foreign affairs,
    care too much about local affairs,
    are at least ten percentage points too cheery of a morning,
    wear the wrong kind of perfume,
    vote the wrong way,
    possess an inordinate number of interest-rate-related insights,
    leave naval-mine-sized key clusters on non-designated shelves,
    usurp power points for hair-drying devices and obsolescent moustache trimmers,
    are indifferent to your variety-specific glassware,
    pronounce sauvignon blanc incorrectly,
    don't see what the big fuss is (about anything),
    disrespect the cutlery drawer,
    disrespect the dishwasher,
    spend a lot of time wondering aloud if anyone else finds it hot in here,
    are very good at noticing your renovation defects,
    purchase margarine when you explicitly asked for butter,
    boil kettles at two o'clock in the morning,
    urinate by electric light at three o'clock in the morning,
    smile empathetically when you re-enter the room after fighting with your spouse,
    smile smugly when you re-enter the room after disciplining your child,
    leave teabags on the sink for reuse at a time that never arrives,

      state opinions you've heard yourself state but in objectively more annoying ways,
      seem not at all impressed by your esteemed job,
        ask questions that suggest they're unsure your esteemed job even is a job,
        are adamant you know whom they're talking about,
        refuse to disengage the button-clicking sound on their smartphones,
        claim to be allergic to all Asian food including rice
        and are yet to decide how long they'll be staying,
are puzzlingly unrelatable.

(After) The Wave

On blissful shorelines
we beach ourselves
whale-slick and exhausted
in the pillowy sand dunes
and drift foamily off to sleep.

Le Déjeuner sur l'Herbe

Praise be
to the plastic prongs and potato salads,
the Norfolk fronds and birthday ballads,
the paper towels, the tartan rugs,
the cooler bags and hay-fever drugs.

Praise be
to the itchy grass and Homebrand Fanta,
the foldout chairs and gormless banter,
the frisbee game, the crying kid,
the leashless dog and leaky lid.

Praise be
to the stumps and the bat and the ball
to the broken thong, to the occupied stall,
the mid-strength beer, the overcooked meat,
the rockmelon wedges and mid-morning heat.

Praise be
to the esky with the missing handles,
the play equipment defaced by vandals,
the bag for food scraps, the portable speaker,
the tomato-sauce stain and dog-shitted sneaker.

Praise be
to the blowflies, mosquitos and bull ants,
the pain-in-the-arse auntie with her pain-in-the-arse rants,
the rival party who nabbed the pergola,
their deadbeat dad with his rum and cola.

Praise be
to the swooping magpies and divebombing plovers,
the discarded condom and absconded lovers,
your welfare-dependant cousin and her latest addition,
your whole dim-witted family and this yearly tradition.

Aboriginal

Thank you, Garry,
for the opportunity to speak
on behalf of Australia's Indigenous community
with this new poem titled 'Aboriginal'.

Before I start,
do you also have a painting called 'Transgender Gaza Hoax'
that I could respond to –
now that I've committed myself to, you know,
permanently decolonising my employment status?

Headland

Wherever it is
I go
during the night,
guided by
the perverse
and angry
totems of
memory and
prophesy of
fear and arousal,
I somehow
never fail
to arrive back
at myself
by morning.

Swollen-handed,
naked, yesterday's
matted beard
sea-weeded across
my neck and
cheeks, visions
of human sacrifice
dangling like
petrified insect
dung from my
eyelashes, I
emerge from that
crumbling sand-
castle of sleep
like some
marauding infidel

still hard with
the taste
of blood and
cunt, wondering
if I really
am
the resurrection
and the
life – or
if that bit
was just a
dream too.

Sentinel

Beware,
a certain breed of psychopath
is drawn to cul-de-sacs like these,
to quiet little dead-end streets
where parents still believe it safe
to send their children out to play
unsupervised in unfenced yards.

Beware,
a certain breed of psychopath
will take his ease among the trees,
the drooping jacaranda trees
that bloom in pleasant purple rows,
while nursing in his blackened heart
sadistic plans for you and yours.

Beware,
a certain breed of psychopath
will wait until your back is turned,
will wait until your stick is down,
will wait until your helmet's off,
your speed reduced, your muscles flagged,
then strike! and strike! and strike again!

Beware,
a certain breed of psychopath
commits such crimes without remorse,
that evil ominous amber eye
unblinking in his frightful head;
he knows his rights, this psychopath,
protected by the wild-life act.

The Cliff

and in it we were naked and
you know　　　having sex
only for some reason we
were on the edge of this enormous
cliff overlooking the ocean and
in it I knew that
as soon as we stopped having
you know　　　stopped making love
that we'd we'd fall off and so
I kept trying to stop myself from
you know　　　from finishing
so that we wouldn't
fall off and and
you know　　　die but
the only way to do this was
to pretend as if I was upset with
her about something to to
act like I was angry with her
which I wasn't I really wasn't but
it was the only way of stopping
myself the only way of of
you know　　　keeping us both alive
but for some reason this started
to become a real sort of
it sounds stupid to say but
a real sort of turn-
on or something for her so
that the more
you know　　　upset I
got in it the more the more
you know　　　the more turned
on she got until
until I could feel myself starting to

I mean actually starting to
get upset with her for for for
real which she just found
hilarious and so started started
you know   laughing her head
off at me and I was trying to
tell her to stop because the
more she laughed the closer
we were getting to the the the edge
and the more upset I
I and I knew if she didn't
stop soon that we
that I that she that we
were going to to to to die for
you know   for for real
like in real life which
is when the kookaburra
this giant yeah this
giant kookaburra I guess it
was just sort of I don't know
appeared on us and it's
hard to explain because it
doesn't really make sense but
it was as if her laughter was
coming out of it or
its laughter was
coming out of her and I I
guess that's when I must
have have woken up or
something because that's
when I reached out to put my
my my my my my my arm
around her and remembered
that she was was was
you know

The Letter

Australia Post
would like to 'hear from me'.

Australia Post
is asking for 'a few minutes of my time'.

Australia Post
has requested feedback on my 'recent delivery experience'.

Australia Post
wants to know 'how likely I am to recommend Australia Post to my friends and family'.

But when I click on <u>the link</u> embedded in the email

from Australia Post, I discover that

Australia Post
isn't accepting qualitative feedback.

Australia Post
is only accepting quantitative feedback.

Australia Post
expects me to rate my recent delivery experience by checking a box between 1 and 10.

Australia Post, my fellow men and women of letters, can no longer be considered an ally to the written word.

The Presence II

A doe and her two bucks,
just this side of the headland.
I spotted them this morning
on my way from visiting your spot.

The doe was reading aloud
and her two bucks were listening.
I was not close enough to hear what,
but, by the libidinous smell in the air,
some poetry-infused declaration of love would be my guess.

If I'd had my rifle with me,
I might have put an end to the scene,
buck-buck-doe: one-two-three,
a slug between each glassy set of eyeballs.

But I did not have my rifle.
I had my paints and paintbrushes.
And so I painted them instead.
A doe, her two bucks, and me,
just this side of wherever you went, my darling.

Dusk

Mount Keira
aka 'Grandmother Mountain'

If you ask me
Mount Keira
looks her most
grandmotherly
when welcoming
and farewelling
the sun
at opposite ends
of the day.

The way
her face
lights up
as he toddles
over the horizon
each morning
with a nuclear
arsenal's worth of
energy to burn.

And then again,
with a certain
rosy hue of
schadenfreude,
as he's being
dragged out
the back door
by the working
parent

who arrives
just in time
for the nightly
meltdown.

The League

Men,
brought together
by smoke, by
the formal agreement
of fire, running now
like rendered fat
through neighbourhood
and nation state,
palms sizzling
with the spit
and blood
and beery lubrications
of adolescent mateship

and the laughter,
that hung
at one good time
from the starchy summer air
like singlets
from Mum's clothesline
or exhaust fumes
from an older brother's
distant tailpipe,
has taken on
a more menacing
tone.

Nightfall

Whose is the night
that bestows fire
with such bright and heretical ambition?

Whose is the night
that terrifies the naked and the old
with its implacable patience and cold, earthy temperament?

Whose is the night
that punctures the skin of day
with a never-ending landscape of fiercely silhouetted teeth?

Whose is the night
that preys on lonely women
with such owl-like precision and such owl-like hunger?

Whose is the night
that drives men to behave so strangely
with such deformities of thought and so dangerous an obedience to this
    thought?

Whose is the night
that separates the inner from the outer
with nothing more judicious than a click of its crow-like tongue?

And whose is the night
that disappears entire mountains, entire oceans, entire hemispheres
simply by laying its shiny blackened eye upon them?

Is it yours,
Kangaroo?

Nightfall II

after Dylan Thomas
but for my dad

Royal North Shore Hospital, February 2024

Not yet, but when the rage calls forth the night
To make its peaceful exit into dark,
Go with it, knowing that you did alright.

Adjust your eyes to the declining light,
Become yourself a minor fading spark,
Not yet, but when the rage calls forth the night.

When you discern it drifting out of sight,
Departing silently without remark,
Go with it, knowing that you did alright.

Avoid the trap of looking back in fright,
Lean boldly forward into your embark.
Not yet, but when the rage calls forth the night

And black becomes definitively bright,
Submit yourself to death's eternal arc.
Not yet, but when the rage calls forth the night,
Go with it, knowing that you did alright.

A Father Is Greater than His Son (fka Firelight)

June to August
During the winter < he would appear in my bedroom doorway each Saturday at the crack of dawn with his liver miraculously regenerated and his thermos full of instant coffee < and off we would go < father and son < to steal a bit of firewood from some quiet country laneway or overgrown stock route on the outskirts of town >> Wielding his Stihl Farm Boss with Promethean defiance < he held little regard for the municipal by-laws and Crown Land signs put in place to keep us separated from those Olympian-sized arseholes down there at Council Chambers < who < with their ducted gas heating < instantaneous boiling water < and salary-induced torpor < constituted the most local and cosily inept of all governmental pantheons >> Mind you < he also held very little regard for the teenage son who < given the choice would have preferred to stay home watching *Rage* and eating Nutri-Grain on the lounge < like some lower-order animal fattening himself for sacrifice < than follow his father < fog-deep < into a paddock full of Scotch thistles < decomposing cow manure and unsplit < would-be fire >>

March to May
In autumn < we dragged pink < headless lures around a dam too
cold to swim in < too empty to waterski on < and too far from
civilisation to escape alone and on foot from >> While we were
not the only father-son duo out there on the clay-coloured snowmelt
at that time of year < it is possible we were the only father-son duo
never < in our hundreds of hours of trying < to successfully extradite
a fish from the condemned township they had flooded to build this
hydro-electrical < outboard-friendly paradise >> To make matters
worse < these other twosomes piloted boats with cool < sexed-up
names like *Milf Hunter* < *Far-Kher* and *Trout Sniffer* < while ours
was an untitled < mustard-yellow Quintrex < equipped with homemade
rod holders and an underpowered Evinrude >> How I used to pray
we would collide with one of the chimney stacks or church steeples
my fluorescent Tassie Devils were forever snagging themselves on
and sink brightly out of sight >>

September to November
Springtime he cleaned and serviced the Triumph motorcycle that had remained more or less unridden since he cut his hair < signed a mortgage and became a dad at age twenty-four >> Like an ex-racehorse that had never managed to place any better than last < the 'Trumpy' was living out its days in an old woodshed at the back of our block < with a canvas coat thrown over its hindquarters for protection against the mice and swallows < and an unregistered < broken-spoked sidecar parked nearby for companionship >> I snuck up there one day after school < while he was at work < with visions of fanging it down the driveway and out of town like some two-wheeled bushranger << I was fifteen years old < beardless and believed < as perhaps all fifteen-year-olds do < that my father was the saddest < most pathetic man alive >> Throwing a black Clarks-shod foot over the saddle < I gave the kick-start everything I had < but was caught off-guard by the decade and a half's worth of recoil stored up in its repressed crankshaft < and thrown clear >>

December to February
Summary was the season of kikuyu grass and dogshit < the ever-converging threat of which he kept at bay with a Victa two-stroke lawnmower built from the remains of half a dozen other Victa two-stroke lawnmowers >> Requiring round-the-clock maintenance and alchemic fuel-to-oil blends < the Victa hated tranquillity with the fire of a thousand mistimed combustions < and resented my father for the life he had so unsympathetically siphoned into it >> Cable-tied < hose-clamped and bound with black electrical tape < it took every opportunity for revenge it got too < blitzing his shins with fragments of dog bone and clothes peg < jettisoning its catcher at the fullest < most histominergically strategic of moments < and blunting its blades against as many concealed concrete surfaces as it could unearth >> Risking life and thumb to unclog its grass chute or pressing his lips to its air filter in a conflicted act of mouth-to-mouth resuscitation < my father could not possibly have imagined the day would come when a son of his would be able to walk into a foreign-owned supermarket and purchase a brushless < battery-powered replacement for under two hundred dollars >> Thank machina he passed away before the latest Aldi catalogue could find its way onto his front lawn >>

39

The Dream

starts out slowly
like milk in a
skull-
sized saucepan
over a low to
medium heat

just a few
sour tendrils
penetrating upward
from a pale
ever-thinning
surface

the heavier
proteins surreptitiously
rearranging
themselves beneath
the surface

good-humouredly
at first like
nothing out of
the ordinary
could possibly be
going on
and then

the second
you drop
your guard / turn
your back

the contents
of the pan
no longer
confined   to the pan

The Guards

*'Neo-Nazis go bush: Grampians gathering highlights
rise of Australia's far right'*
     Sydney Morning Herald, *27 January 2021*

'White pride! White power! Heil Hitler!' the
lads can be heard chanting as they pump their
way through the night, painting the Grampians
white with jerry can after jerry can of the steroid-
infused semen they've been stock-piling since
Great-Grandfather Brutus returned from the
United Nations with his hard-on tucked between his
legs and his wallet crammed full of Jew Glue. Hour
after hour, they flog themselves stupid, these
good and godly lads, as tireless and loyal as
blisters on a ball sack, they are, with nothing
but the upside-down fires of foreign idolatry to
keep them from falling into the deserted and treacherous
mineshafts the culturati insist on calling "History".
Self-appointed defenders of the shoreline, self-
anointed protectors of the bloodline, direct descendants
of Simpson's mighty donkey, they've pledged to
secure a racially purified future for the sake of their
unborn white grandkids by coming up trumps
where The New Guard et al. pulled up stumps. And so
is it any bloody wonder they should have felt the
need to trek all the way up here into the Victorian high
country to do so? With ambitions as soggy as these,
only a Grampian-sized Sao could possibly suffice!

New Land

Australian place names beginning with 'New':

New Auckland, QLD. New Beith, QLD. New Berrima, NSW. New Brighton, NSW. New Buildings, NSW. New Chum, QLD. New Farm, QLD. New Gisborne, VIC. New Harbourline, QLD. New Italy, NSW. New Lambton, NSW. New Lambton Heights, NSW. New Mapoon, QLD. New Mexico, NSW. New Moonta, QLD. New Norcia, WA. New Norfolk, TAS. New Park, NSW. New Port, SA. New Residence, SA. New Town, SA. New Town, TAS. New Valley, NSW. New Well, SA. Newbold, NSW. Newborough, VIC. Newbridge, NSW. Newbridge, VIC. Newbury, VIC. Newcarlbeon, WA. Newcastle, NSW. Newcastle East, NSW. Newcastle Waters, NT. Newcastle West, NSW. Newcomb, VIC. Newdegate, WA. Newee Creek, NSW. Newell, QLD. Newfield, VIC. Newham, VIC. Newhaven, VIC. Newington, NSW. Newington, VIC. Newland, SA. Newlands, QLD. Newlands, WA. Newlands Arm, VIC. Newlyn, VIC. Newlyn North, VIC. Newman, WA. Newmarket, QLD. Newmerella, VIC. Newnes, NSW. Newnes Plateau, NSW. Newnham, TAS. Newport, NSW. Newport, VIC. Newport, QLD. Newport Beach, NSW. Newry, VIC. Newrybar, NSW. Newstead, NSW. Newstead, VIC. Newstead, QLD. Newstead, TAS. Newton, SA. Newton Boyd, NSW. Newtown, NSW. Newtown, VIC. Newtown, VIC. Newtown, QLD. Newtown, QLD.

Recite them quickly enough and it sounds almost nonsensical.

The Antipodes

talk about wrong-footed

I knew a guy
who hit an emu
with his ute
on the way to a B&S ball
out near Narrabri somewhere

thinking it'd be funny
he propped the dead bird up
in the passenger seat
next to him
pulled the seatbelt across
and continued on
to the ball

when he got to the gate
he wound down his window
and like a real clever cunt
said to the ticket lady
'yeah, two tickets please'
wink wink nod nod

which is about
when the emu
came back to life
and starting kicking
all manner of shit
out of him and
the WB's leather upholstery

wasn't dead see
just stunned or something
anyway long story short
everyone ended up
getting real drunk
and having a pretty
decent night regardless

(except this other
random bloke
who got run over
in his swag
by some unit
doing circle work
in the middle
of the night
and ended up
dying poor cunt)

The Rainbow

after William Wordsworth
(and Albury)

It was a rainbow in the sky
that led Kangaroo to proclaim:
    'The Child is father of the Man'.

My four-year-old son
needed no such sign when
from his spot at the breakfast table
he looked out through the kitchen window and announced:
    'It's a big day, today, Dad.'

With my eyes on my emails,
I responded as any father might:
    'Why, what have we got on today?'

He shook his small, peripheral head,
pointed his spoon and with
a Cornflakey drawl explained:
    'No, not like that. That's not what I mean.
    I mean the day. It's big. *Really* big. Look!'

And, lo and behold, he was right,
was Kangaroo:
    The Child truly *is* father of the Man.

The Cockies

Cast out of the escarpment
with thunderous verdict,
they come screeching
through the afternoon suburb
like quashed seraphim,
their heads ablaze
and their wings shuddering
with downward thrust
           and seditious thrill.

To the hellhouse!
To the hellhouse!
at the end of the street,
where they'll swing
by wicked nail and gnarly beak
from ruined flyscreens and rotted joists,
like idiot demons, hyenic and brash,
or after-school eshays
           scrounging for cash.

Flaming Kangaroo

This painting has had me thinking of my brother-in-law, who has been a part-time firefighter for several years now. To become a part-time firefighter, you have to make it through two weeks of intense training. According to my brother-in-law, it is not especially difficult to make it through the two weeks of intense training, but the instructors do show you and tell you some pretty awful things during those two weeks. According to my brother-in-law, they show you and tell you these awful things in order to prepare you for the job, which, of course, makes sense. One of the more horrific things related to my brother-in-law by his instructors and, in turn, related to me by my brother-in-law, concerns house fires and deceased children. If you do not want to know what they tell you at firefighter training concerning housefires and deceased children, then you should stop reading here. Because this prose poem is not a work of fiction. The awful thing they tell you at firefighter training concerning house fires and children is real. I can independently verify it is real because I tried using it in a work of fiction once, a short story, and it just would not go. It was too real for that fictitious story inasmuch as it had the effect of turning all the other details in the story to ash. So, I am using it here instead. This single real thing. But again, believe me when I tell you that it is a terrible thing to know. And if you do not want to know it, then you should take my advice and stop reading immediately. Because what they tell you is that if you enter into a house that is on fire and cannot find the children that are supposed to be inside, and if you can hear the mother screaming at you from the front lawn to save her *babies* — because this is what she will be calling them, regardless their ages, with the neighbours holding her by the hair to stop her from running back in there herself — then you should go immediately to the kitchen and check the refrigerator. Apparently, this is where many children go to escape the heat in the case of a house fire. They are drawn from their beds and through the flames by some desperate atavism, telling them to go to where it is cold. They burrow in like marsupials, clawing food items from shelves and shelves from shelf-holders. If they are lucky, they fall asleep in there and suffocate. It is difficult to imagine anybody falling asleep inside a refrigerator during a housefire, but apparently it is possible. If they are unlucky, the heat catches up to them and burns them alive inside the refrigerator, cooking the remaining items of food in the process. This is what was related to my brother-in-law during his two weeks of firefighter training and what, in turn, he related to me. A truly horrifying image. Too horrifying for fiction, as I have already noted. But one that has come to me again in the middle of this second coronavirus lockdown and left me wondering if, when it is all over and done with, we will find parks and ovals and cycleways full of dead children, children who woke during the night and, responding to some innate instinct they themselves could not possibly have understood, fled their beds in search of a cool, open space.

Creation

What shameful invention does Man suffer,
plucked from the earth like a wrinkled parsnip
with clods of dirt still coughing and crapping
their way free of him for decades after.

If he's lucky, the world will eat him alive,
grow strong on whatever morsels of protein
he manages to drag up through the soil
on his way into the piercing, photosynthetic light.

Any less fortunate though, and it's straight for the kitchen scrap bowl,
let the chickens and worms wrap their digestive juices
around a bit of that vitamin-G goodness Sister Sentience
has been pumping him full of all this evolutionary while.

And let's not forget poor old Mother Earth in all this either,
whose loamy undulations and tectonic readjustments
barely raise a seismographic eyebrow down there
on the ward of relative contraction and quantum concern.

Nothing but a self-entitled pain in the backside
if you ask the Big Obstetrician in the sky.
Mind you, he's been on duty for around 4.6 billion years now,
so is probably just crabby on account of being cosmically overtired.

Save your sermons and give it to us straight, Kangaroo:
is this really it, your telestic vision manifest?
Or are you as mystified by the whole micro-bacterial, macro-ethereal
shitshow as the rest of us vegetable-brained degenerates,
wondering why we were uprooted in the first place,
if only to wither and die?

The Dance

Two male roos
fighting over a mate

resemble a pair of treble clefs
squaring off over a stave

their heads pulled back
all their weight on their tails

it'd pass for dancing
if they could agree on a time signature.

The Awakening

Now arrive the animals,
to watch the way we do it:
Man and Woman, Woman and Man
holding fast to one another in the reciprocal authority
and thornless husbandry
of an afternoon's lovely intercourse.

What must they be thinking, Kangaroo and Bird,
sidled up to and perched upon the balustrade
like a pair of timid first-time orgy-goers
who are pretty sure but not a hundred per cent sure but pretty sure
they have the right address?

Come one, come all?!?
Is this what goes through their animal minds
as they watch us work our way toward
conjoint achievement on the cottage veranda where
the miracles of human love and courtly expression prove
only half as useful to our lascivious cause as
the miracle of opposable thumbs?

Or do they not even have minds?
Are they here purely for the pheromones?
Descended from the rocky enclaves and leafy
bordellos of the nearby escarpment because they
smelt a bit of screw in the air and wanted in-
out, in-out on the action?

Lower-order animals watching higher-order animals mate:
that's what we have here.
Mind you, they did not bring this scene of depravity upon themselves
no way no how, not in a million-plus years of evolution.

All the time in the world to develop deviances
as deep and diagnosable as our own
and they still don't even have a word for 'non-reproductive coitus'
these poor bipedal innocents.

So, let them take in a bit of human culture then!
Why the hell not?
Let this grand spectacle we created for the betterment of our species
draw them in and derange them with its sighs and rubbings,
its grunts and unbuttonings, with the fantastical
rigidity of its desires and the energising, everlasting warmth
of its returns.

Let them inch marginally closer with each compression too,
Ah-ha, ah-ha, that's it, that's it, that's it…
their shadows lengthening toward us as they observe
the mutual and often vulgar urgency by which
we arrange ourselves in so many ostensibly hostile positions.

Let them study the warped accelerations
and unstable radii of our leaky embraces
smell the thick dingo-like fragrance that
emanates from our armpits and the backs of our knees
as we near yet another awkward and shaky completion.

Have them do so not for our benefit but
for the betterment of their own species,
that they may take this newly acquired knowledge
(knowledge we invented!)
back to the rocky enclaves and leafy bordellos of the nearby escarpment
and disseminate it among their peers like some
ecstatic instruction manual covered in lewd scribblings
and prelusive adulterated discharges.
Have it run amok amongst them as it has run amok amongst us,

for it truly is as close a thing as there is in this world to pure, animal delight.

the awakening ii

looks like another
marginal afternoon

on the horizon
for this pair of freshly

awoken bedfellows
their shadows barely

emerged from the
thickets of morning

lengthening now
toward the sky's ever-

receding light source
like soft-pawed

animals too tired and
thirsty to resist

the earth's happy
orbit any longer

and so what
if they refuse

or prove unable
to hold their shape

in the face
of the whirling

centrifuges of time
even love yields

to this most universal
and peculiar of laws:

the attraction
of opposites

The Envoy

To watch
while your wife
is administered
from behind
by a fully erect
kangaroo is
to experience
the whole-
sale power
of God's
warped diplomacy.

To suggest
opening a window
after the fact,
like your wife
were an
embassy guestroom,
is to
demonstrate the
ineptitude of
soft-power
politics in
what is essentially
a hard-
power cosmos.

Noon

In the colder months,
Friday noon is the best
time of the week
for lovemaking.

The quilted mattress
is a garden bed of warmth
into which we bury ourselves,
naked but for socks.

The sun shining in
through the slatted blind
germinates the fine hairs
that grow from a patch
of stomach just kissed, from
the thigh wet with breath.

And afterwards we
lie like children home
sick from school, our
cheeks blotched with
fever and the weekend
wide ahead of us.

Treason

for Boyd

Or then there was the time
when I declined to stand with
the rest of the green-and-gold-
scarved crowd (even the friend
I'd come with, the one with the full-
time job who'd paid for my ticket)
because I'd got the idea under my
mortarboard on our way from the
lecture theatre to the stadium, yes,
under that tasselled laurel crown I
used to clothe my mind with, that
nationhood was nothing to crow
about, was nothing to sing about,
was nothing to go getting a right-
wing glow about, was just this, well,
imaginary construct thing no doubt
like all those other imaginary constructy
things I'd been taught to flout by some
Frenchman whose name I took great
care in pronouncing right, in pro-
nouncing *juste comme ça*, because
getting the accents wrong would
have been even more embarrassing
to me than the piss that declined
to leave my bladder as I stood shoulder-
to-shoulder after the final whistle with
a trough line of patriotic and joyful
Wallabies supporters who found the
praxis of relieving themselves in
public no more difficult than knowing
when to stand the fuck up and sing.

The Secret

Do children in China
play a game called Australian Whispers?

And is the object of that game
to dress up as readily identifiable Australian fauna
and see which ALP members they can fool
into divulging national secrets?

And did the former ALP senator
forced to resign from parliament
over accusations he provided Chinese billionaires
with counter-surveillance advice,
ever manage to convince the leader
of the One Nation Party
to eat that Halal Snack Pack
he was always cajoling her with?

Or did the leader of the One Nation Party
smell the Islamo-Chinese influence
on her ALP counterpart
(they say she had a nose for oxymoronic treachery)
and go running for the shelter
of her Queensland prison cell?

And will the answers to such questions
even matter a hundred years from now
when Queensland has been renamed
Generalsecretarysland and all the kangaroos
have been replaced with panda bears
under the direction of the next century's
Leader for Life?

Maybe. Maybe not.
Depends who you listen to.
And who they've been listening to.
And whether any of them are fans
of xenomoronic poetry.

The Intruder ★ ★ ★ ★ ☆
(PG) 100 minutes, Wyewurk Theatre

The star of the film, Skippy, an eastern grey kangaroo with a weakness for black jelly beans, finds herself caught between a rock and a hard place when long-time love interest, Clarissa, is brutally assaulted in her beachside home by a man known only as The One-Eyed Rapist. Operating under twin clouds of suspicion, Skippy must decide whether she will risk jumping through fire in an effort to bring The One-Eyed Rapist to justice or save herself from further suspicion and likely incarceration by escaping on a high-powered speed boat. Fans of the original *Skippy the Bush Kangaroo* TV series will undoubtedly appreciate special cameo performances from David Herbert Lawrence and Garry James Shead, who play a pair of bumbling wildlife smugglers seeking to profit from Clarissa's assault by forcing her to carry the baby full-term so that they can auction it to the highest bidder on the ethically dubious international art market. With school holidays just around the corner, you'd be hopping mad to miss this one.

Marriage

Marriage is a pair of magpies amusing
Themselves by seeing how long they
Can hop in tandem on one leg without
Needing to flap their wings for balance or
Flying away bored. Marriage is a three-
Legged kangaroo hiding its extra limb
Inside its tail so as not to arouse the
Suspicion or envy of the other marsupials
Nor catch the attention of the sun god
Who sends his firstborn child to earth
In the form of a soft-bearded bushfire every
Second or third Boxing Day. Marriage is an
Unconsummated bedsheet of clear blue
Sky hidden behind a veil of yellowing
Chantilly cloud cover and rising eucalyptus
Fumes from the factory of invasive
Species and sick familial love. Marriage
Is a diprotodon hunted to extinction by a
Bridal party of eloping sex addicts from
Europe who arrived here broke and will
Leave punch-drunk with their pockets
Full of chlamydia. Marriage is the sand-
Stone precipice from which we hurl
Boulders at those scrounging around for
Earthworms and bugs in the long, ageing
Shadow of this here mountain a few of us
Are still happy to call 'home sweet home'.

Checkmate

War ponies whinnying about like clockwork vultures
driven wild by the smell of their own emasculated panic;

thin-faced, stiletto-hatted assassins stabbing blindly at each other
with their long arms and sleek Pythagorean compass blades;

a trench full of clubfooted invalids with nothing more
glorious on their minds than making it out alive;

identical twin brothers caught behind the line of
razor wire they so obediently but so stupidly erected;

some tough old bitch in her nightgown hurling grenades
at the passing tanks from her second-storey balcony;

and the semi-impotent imbecile who started this whole thing
hiding in the corner at the bottom of a stairwell with his crown on back-
    to-front.

Checkmate II

Some dads beat their
sons with straps, some
with canes and some
with belts, some use
telephone directories
(to prevent the welts),
hell, some even resort
to their bare fists
when there's literally
nothing else at hand.
My old man, the sick
prick, got his kicks by
beating me into shape
with a pair of rooks and
an encyclopaedic array
of exchange-variation
e4 opening attack lines.

Each evening, with the
dishes washed, dried
and shelved and piano
practice out of the way,
he'd have me accompany
him to his den (the
half of the garage he'd
partitioned, carpeted
and lined with books),
where I was forced to
choose between two
tightly closed sets of
knuckles. If I picked

the row concealing
the white piece, that
shiny princely figurine,
whose head he'd thumbed
to the highest of sheens,
he'd smile and warn
me not to blow the
lead. If I selected
the hand harbouring
the darker piece though,
with its glum green-
felted base and b-flat
personality, he'd get
a cruel, mad glint
in his eye and I'd know
I was in for a terrible
and violent thrashing.

I didn't recognise it
at the time, of course
(too caught up in the
parallels of self-pity
and adolescence, in
my own intersecting
irrationalities and L-
shaped uncertainties),
but I see it clearly now:
those nightly hammerings,
those stilted, set-piece
humiliations didn't ruin
me or condemn me to
a lifetime of incapacity
and failure; they were
lessons, you see, in

manhood and resilience,
from a father to his son,
which I credit for all the
successes I have today:
a loving wife, a rewarding
job, a beautiful home
and my own pawn-
faced bundle of joy, who
at just three and a half
years of age (he still
calls it 'chest', god love
him) supplies me with
all the retribution a man
could possibly ask for.

The Supper

Now it is the appointed Time, the Hour at which Man and Bird and Beast are brought together through a Convocation of Labour and Labour's prime Reward; where Sacrificer and Sacrificee, still fragrant with the Blood of Morning and Harvest, gather by twisted Beak and crooked Hand to acknowledge that the Conditions of Honour and Hunger have been met for a fifth or fifteenth Night in a Row; where it has become customary for them to drink Port Wine from unleavened Barrels of dead Swine Gut and dead Oak Tree and melted Beeswax and to remedy their collective Misfortune with the cutting of Meats and sowing of Teeth; where each Participant here has a Name and where each Name is an Order of Animal derived according to the ancient Hierarchy of Famine that names and consumes all living Things; where the Door and Window of the Room in which they supper have been flung open to allow their Evening's Prayer an easy Escape through the irreverent and oppressive Geometry of Lighting that characterises their Mood as it characterises their unstoppable Passage through History; that they may witness it fly outwards toward a God who is neither real nor there, just a Patch of Sky filled with Benevolence, Humour and Divine Mystery and who, in turn, fills the Earth's eternal Stomach with equal Measures of Light and Shadow, Drought and Flood, Satiety and Satiety's grand Opposite.

The Meeting

There's indecision in the air this evening
and it's undermining the astro-celestial quo:
the moon is lacking in confidence,
the stars appear unsure of whose turn it is next
and the sun is questioning whether or not
it made the right decision in the first place.

There's indecision in the air this evening
and it's affecting the behaviour of animals and people alike:
the neighbours are enjoying a game of Marco Polo
in their new above-ground swimming pool while Frank, our sausage dog,
stands half inside, half outside, barking at them through the cat flap.

There's indecision in the air this evening
and it's giving me bad vibes which I can't quite put my finger on:
like when you think you might have been caught
by a speed camera or red light camera
but won't know for sure until the fine does or doesn't arrive
in the mail sometime soon or sometime never.

There's indecision in the air this evening
and it's wreaking havoc with the upstairs plumbing:
strata are saying they'll have someone out here first thing in the morning
but they aren't saying where we're supposed to relieve ourselves
between now and then.

There's indecision in the air this evening
and just one thing for it:
a family meeting to decide which kid lives
and which kid we sacrifice in the hope our petty and equivocating God
might piss off back to Paradise and leave us in peace for a bit.

Death of Cooley

In all of Jerusalem
and in all of Judea
and in all of Samaria
laughs the Kookaburra.
Hotblooded progenitor of antipodal delirium,
full-throated, feather-throated father
of innumerable miraculous ecstasies,
swallower of worms,
alighter of backyard swing sets,
diviner of lightning storms and other cloudy-scented optimisms,
come down from your eucalyptic throne-top
and penetrate me with your mirth,
split me up the middle with your obscene sense of humour
before warbling me to climax with that Christ-sized bill of yours
and leaving me pinned
crucified
      satisfied
           revivified
to the morning's electricity pole.

O, Kookaburra,
Holy Dove of the Illawarra,
what insane fantasies you fill me with,
whipping horses from my flesh like sweat,
sucking paint from my armpits and along my distant cliff faces,
beating snakes from my sandy bushes with your colourful imperialism
and strange Irish ancestry.

O, Kookaburra,
descendent of Abraham, Isaac and Jacob,
of David, Heli and Joseph,
what hazy and indulgent prophesies might you convince me of now

in this hour of cerulean immaculacy and deep,
deep ekphrastic hallucination?
Kookaburra,
 O Kookaburra,
 O Kookaburra,
Merry-Merry King of Men Are Thee!

Death of Kangaroo

How brutal the bullet of grief that did this,
that crucified Kangaroo:
blasphemed marsupial of the scrub paddock and border paddock,
of escarpments and roadways and golf courses too.

What velocity the hammer of authority's instinct must possess,
to plough so greyly into the earth
this cross-starred apostle of such hind-legged summit
and such wheat-eating girth.

Was it you again, Pilate,
with your lead-tipped whip and your clean hands and impossible power?
Or perhaps it was the high priest of the paintbrush,
hiding away now in his wide-brimmed hat, and triangle of guilt and glower.

Ah, put down your instruments of passion, Shead,
and accept what is done, and what is done, and what is dead.
Quit your memories and your proclivities and the sources of your similes
and step forward, man, with your pockets out-turned and your excuses
    unexplored.

For unholy, unholy, unholy, unholy are the relics continuously cut
from the eternal carcass of this narrow-jawed saint,
delivered through the tomblike opening of his mother's womb,
only to be airlinered and parliamented, court-housed and coined,
colonised with filament, panel and paint.

No, I say this to you and to all,
for the forgiveness of sins fared seafully
from imperial coastline to most bastardised shore:
Lift Up Your Hearts And Pray Pardon To The Land Which Is God,
for the blood of the bushfire is new and everlasting

and only It may rightfully forget or undo
— *a morte iniquitatis Macropus* —
this iniquitous death of Kangaroo.

The Monument

Let Kangaroo, that fierce and fearless mother of history,
lower her flags and banners and mourn today,
for today our continent is a continent overshadowed by grief,
overcome and obliterated by memories of young heroes,
whose sorrowing sweethearts do once again flock
by chime of townhall clock to school and beach and public park,
where they may honour her losses and soften her deeds with their silence.

Let Kangaroo, that usually gladsome and enduring master of ceremonies,
never shy or short of a joke, always wry, spry and ready to poke, stand
motionless and spiry as a charred fence post at dawn,
her galvanised stare still bolted to the smouldering horizon
were it a hillside of little wooden crosses planted along the smooth and regal
bosom of tomorrow's unborn queen.

Let Kangaroo, that handsome and excited chap from next door,
who thinks the sepia-toned portrait of herself in uniform
was worth the price of admission alone,
discover just how heart-wrenchingly photogenic she really is;
have them shoot her from every which way from
every which angle from every which vantage point,
have them shoot her in the back when she isn't looking,
have them shoot her in the front when she is,
have them shoot her in trenches and fields and on beaches and in mud and
then ship her muddy bloody body home so that we can shoot her some more
and some more and some more, until the only thing keeping her from
falling over stone-cold dead is the cache of bullets bursting
outwards through her beautiful, boyish skin.

Let the sculptor's dream become the taxidermist's worst nightmare,
lest any of us ever forget.

Main Street

in memory of Lawrence Hargrave (Drive)

With your high-school achievement award in mathematics,
your experiential passion for circumnavigation,
your adequate inheritance and your moderate competency,
you defied the odds and transformed yourself into a 50km/h main street.

It might have been ambitious and risky, needlessly dumb,
like agreeing to sit in the exit-row seat of that homemade box kite,
but it proved once and for all that with a steamroller attitude
(and a few thousand wheelbarrow loads of hot mix premium-grade asphalt),

it is possible for a man to quite literally put himself on the map.

The Apotheosis of D.H. Lawrence

No miracle required to resurrect
Those holy sons and daughters who entomb
Themselves while still alive in crypts bedecked

With gilded text and visions that subsume
Them whole. No miracle required to roll
Away the clothbound stone that seals the room

Where lie preserved, in spirit and in soul,
Those hallowed sons whom age does not degrade,
Those hallowed daughters death cannot control.

No miracle required, no offering made,
No prayer or plea or desperate bid will speed
Them forward, those sons and daughters who evade

By art their mortal dues; the only deed
One need endeavour is to sit and read.

Acknowledgements

This collection began with an in situ reading at Wollongong Art Gallery in 2017. My thanks to gallery staff Vivian Vidulich, Louise Brand and John Monteleone, who leant their support (and paintings) at various points along the way. Thank you to my colleagues at UOW (past and present), especially Catherine McKinnon, Sue Bennett, Peter Kelly, Jo Law, Teo Treloar, Aaron Burton, Phillippa Webb, Jo Stirling, Joshua Lobb, Madeleine Kelly, Shady Cosgrove, Christine Howe, Emma Darragh, Alan Wearne, Stephanie Perrett, Hall Murray, Mohammad Makki, Grant Ellmers, Katrina Gamble, Stacie Sims, Nikki Easterbrook and Vasileios Vasileaiadis. Thank you to Joseph Davis for sharing your inexhaustible expertise on Lawrence and the Illawarra. Thank you to Jake Goetz for reading and suggesting improvements, and for the endorsement. Thank you to Mark Mordue for the thoughtful words. Thank you to Suzy Freeman-Greene for publishing the Kangaroo Unbound essay in *The Conversation*. A big thank you to David Musgrave at Puncher and Wattmann for getting behind the work. My love and gratitude to Mara, my first and favourite reader. And to our/my five children, who LOVE poetry readings more than anything else in the world :-) Thank you to Roseanne Shead for your help and support, and to Garry Shead for your generosity, vision and divine being.

The poems 'The Supper' and 'Death of Kangaroo' were first published in *Griffith Review*. 'Death of Cooley' was first published in *Unlikely: Journal for Creative Arts*. 'Flaming Kangaroo' was first published in *Island Online*.

'They Were There' takes the phrase 'ciggy butt brain' from Michael Cusack's animated cartoon of the same name (available on YouTube).

'Free' takes the lines 'You feel free in Australia. There is great relief in the atmosphere' from D.H. Lawrence's 1923 novel *Kangaroo*.

'The Struggle' is a found poem, built on text taken from Maurizio Meloni's essay 'A Triangle of Thoughts: Girard, Freud, Lacan', published in issue 14 of the *European Journal of Psychoanalysis*, 2002.

'Nightfall' owes a debt to Ted Hughes's poem 'Examination at the Womb Door', 'Nightfall II' to Dylan Thomas's poem 'Do Not Go Gentle into That Good Night', and 'Thirroulia' to Anne Sexton's poem 'The Starry Night.'

'The Rainbow' takes the line 'The Child is father of the Man' from William Wordsworth's poem 'My Heart Leaps Up'.

'The Intruder' takes some inspiration from Lee Robinson's 1969 film *Skippy and the Intruders.*

'The Monument' takes numerous words and phrases from a 1923 ANZAC Day column published in *The Age* newspaper.

Finally, it would not have been possible to write or even conceive of this suite of poems without the existence of Sasha Grishin's 1994 monograph *Garry Shead: the D.H. Lawrence Paintings*. What a gift that book has been.

Luke Johnson is a writer and academic from Wollongong, NSW. His poems, stories, essays and criticism are widely published in Australia and have won or been listed for numerous national prizes, including the AAWP Chapter One Prize, the Elizabeth Jolley Award, the Josephine Ulrick Award and the Katharine Susannah Prichard Award as well as several development fellowships. He is the author of the short story collection *Ferocious Animals* (Recent Work Press 2021) and a senior lecturer in creative writing at the University of Wollongong.

www.ingramcontent.com/pod-product-compliance
Ingram Content Group UK Ltd.
Pitfield, Milton Keynes, MK11 3LW, UK
UKHW031103170325
456354UK00003B/277